More Spanish for Little Girls

A Spanish language workbook for little girls

Written and Illustrated by: Yvonne Crawford

www.languageforlittlelearners.com

ISBN 978-0-9844548-6-0

About this workbook

This book is a continuation of Spanish for Little Girls. In this second level your daughter will continue her exploration of the Spanish language while engaging in activities that will help to motivate her. She will pretend to be a baby animal, dress up like a fairy, play with paper dolls, and more.

This workbook is created especially for parents who do not have any prior knowledge of Spanish. You and your daughter can embark on a journey of learning a foreign language together. Everything you need is inside this workbook, including a pronunciation guide, dictionary and teaching hints.

Every lesson will consist of a list of vocabulary words with pictures, three activities your daughter can do in the workbook with your guidance and two activities you can do together without the workbook for further practice. Each new word that is introduced will have its pronunciation next to it.

In the appendices there is a learning slide that your daughter can color after she completes each lesson. This will help your child to visualize and take pride in her progress.

Try not to put stress on your daughter to have perfect pronunciation or to remember every single word. If she forgets a word, simply repeat it and then use it in a sentence a few times; eventually she will catch on. It is important for her (and you) to have a positive first experience with learning a foreign language. It will encourage her to continue and succeed in the future with more language studies.

Table of Contents

Lección 1

Art Girls

Vocabulary:

la artista *lah-ahr-**tees**-tah*
artist

la escultora
*lah-ehs-kool-**toh**-rah*
sculptor

el cepillo de pintura
*ehl-say-**pee**-yoh-day-peen-**too**-rah*
paint brush

la pintora *lah-peen-**tohr**-ah*
painter

la pintura *lah-peen-**too**-rah*
paint

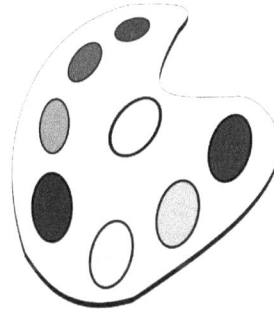

el lápiz *ehl-**lah**-pees*
pencil

Fun Phrases:

sí	*see*	yes
no	*noh*	no
quizás	*kee-**sahs***	maybe

Teaching Tips:

- Throughout the day, ask your children questions in either Spanish or English and then prompt them to answer you in Spanish with the words they learned above for yes, no and maybe.

- If your child asks you what a word is in Spanish that is not listed in this book, look it up in a Spanish/English dictionary or on a website and then create a little dictionary for them out of a small spiral notebook. You can even have them draw the picture in order to help them to remember the word.

Actividad Uno

¡*Hola*! My name is María. It's nice to meet you. Can you match the picture to the correct Spanish word?

la escultora

la pintora

la artista

Actividad Dos

Now you can greet each of my friends in Spanish! For each picture above, say '*Hola*', then say their name.

Actividad Tres

Tell me which of these things you like. If you like them then write sí and if you don't like them write *no*.

Me gusta... I like...

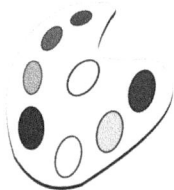

_____

- - - - - - - - - -

_____

_____

- - - - - - - - - -

_____

_____

- - - - - - - - - -

_____

_____

- - - - - - - - - -

_____

_____

- - - - - - - - - -

_____

Actividad Cuatro

Yes, No, or Maybe?

Throughout the day, use your Spanish whenever you can! When your mom or dad asks you a question, say the answer in Spanish. Use: sí, *no*, or *quizás*. Every time you say one of these words today, you can come back to this workbook and record it on this page. Color a star each time you use one of your new Spanish words.

sí   *no*   *quizás*

☆ ☆ ☆ ☆ ☆ ☆ ☆ ☆ ☆

Actividad Cinco

Pencil Toss

What you will need:
construction paper
scissors
pencil
cardboard
cap or cup

What to do:
1. Draw and cut out 10 pencils. You can trace the one from the workbook if you would like.
2. Glue the cut-out pencils to the cardboard and get your mother or father to help you cut them out.
3. Toss the pretend pencils into the cap or cup and count them in Spanish as you do. *un lápiz, dos lápices,* etc.

Lección 2
Silly Faces

Vocabulary:

el pelo *ehl-pay-loh*
hair

la cara *lah-kah-rah*
face

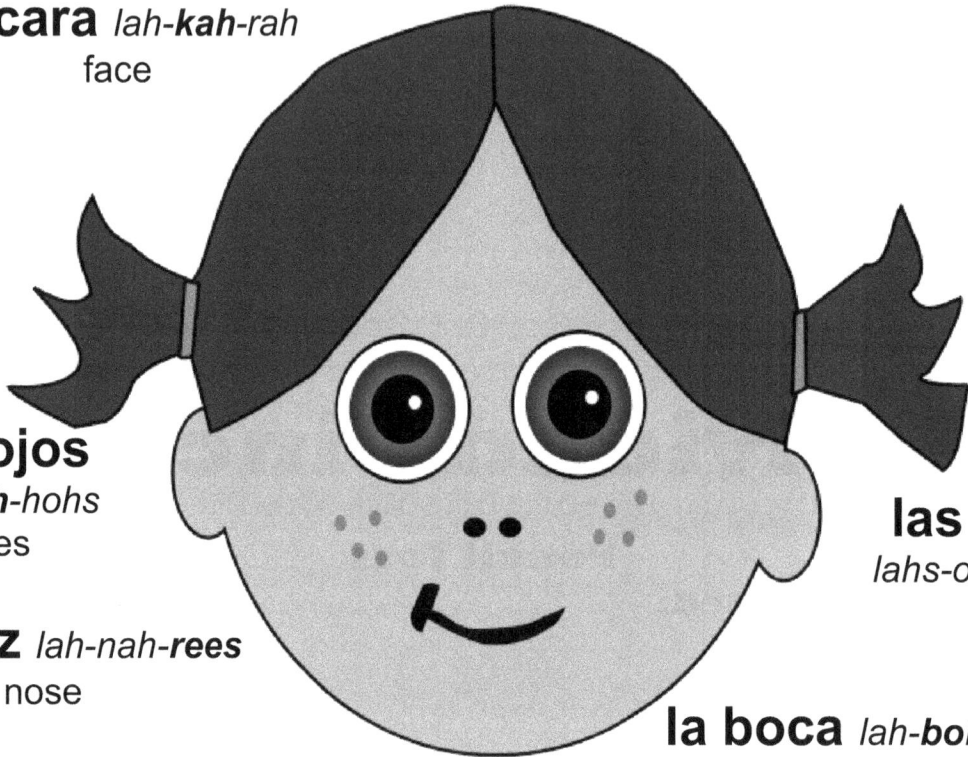

los ojos
lohs-oh-hohs
eyes

las orejas
lahs-oh-ray-hahs
ears

la nariz *lah-nah-rees*
nose

la boca *lah-boh-kah*
mouth

estoy enojada
eh-stoy-ay-noh-hah-dah
I'm angry

estoy loca
eh-stoy-loh-kah
I'm crazy

estoy triste
*eh-**stoy**-**trees**-tay*
I'm sad

estoy feliz
*eh-**stoy**-fay-**lees***
I'm happy

Fun Phrases:

muy	**moo**-ee	very

Teaching Tips:

- Go through the lessons as fast or as slow as your child wants to go. Look to her for signs of fatigue. There is always tomorrow where you can take up where you left off today.

- Feel free to go back to the first level of Spanish for Little Girls in case your daughter has forgotten things like colors or numbers in Spanish. It's a good idea to go back and review previous topics.

Actividad Uno

Come and meet some of my friends. Each of them is missing one part of their faces. Say the name of the facial part that is missing in Spanish and then draw the missing parts on their face.

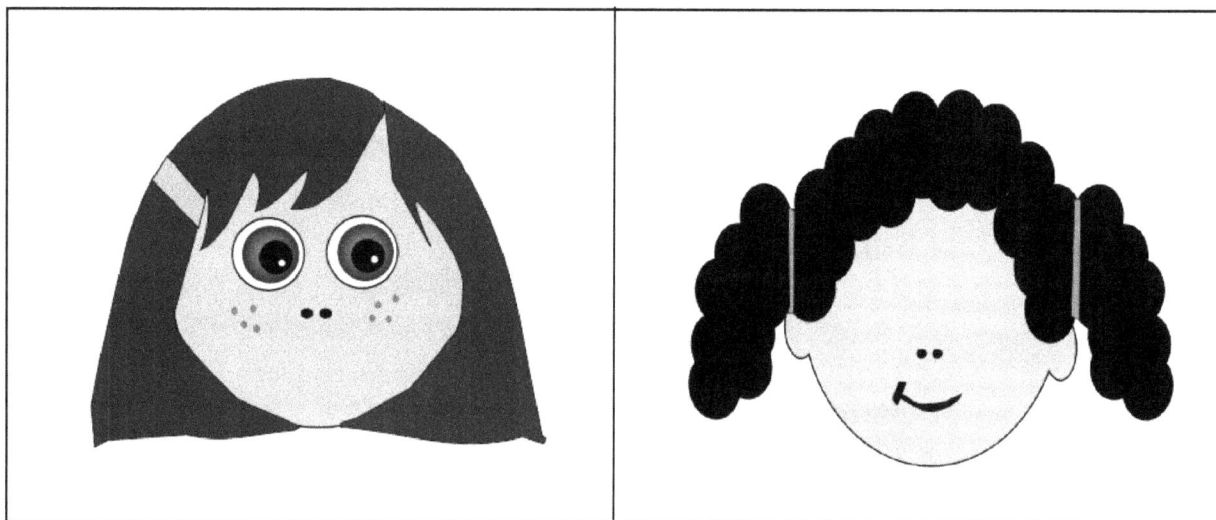

Actividad Dos

Oh no, one of my friends had to go away on vacation and she was supposed to spend the day with me. Can you draw me a friend? As you draw the different body and facial parts, say their names in Spanish. Make sure to use colors and say the colors' names in Spanish too.

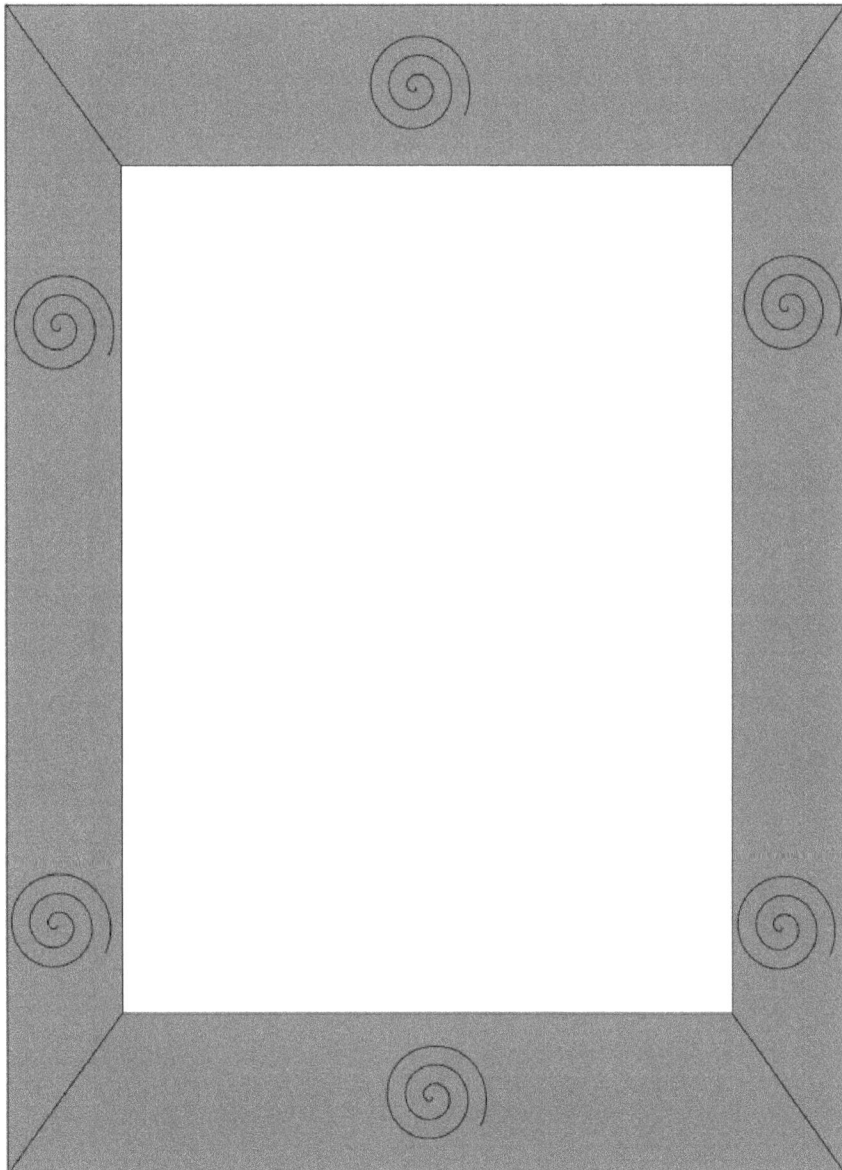

Actividad Tres

Match the Spanish word to the correct facial picture.

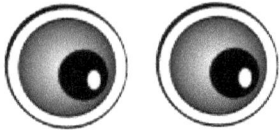

las orejas

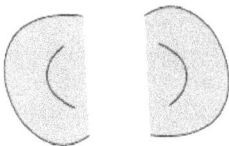

el pelo

la nariz

los ojos

la boca

Actividad Cuatro

Drawing Faces

What you will need:

paper
pencil

What to do:

1. Draw one facial part on a piece of paper.
2. Have your siblings or parents guess what it is. Tell them the name in Spanish.
3. Switch roles; now you guess what they are drawing. Say the word in Spanish.
4. Keep on playing, switching roles after each turn.

Actividad Cinco

Different Faces

What you will need:

your mom, dad or sibling

What to do:

1. Your mom or dad will make a face.
2. In Spanish describe how the face is. Is it a sad face? A mad face? A crazy face? If so, say the names in Spanish.
3. Switch roles with your parent. Now, it is your turn to make silly faces and your parents can describe them in Spanish.

Lección 3

Dress Up

Vocabulary:

las joyas *lahs-**hoh**-yahs*
jewelry

el collar *ehl-koh-**lahr***
necklace

la pulsera
*lah-pool-**say**-rah*
bracelet

el anillo *ehl-ah-**nee**-yoh*
ring

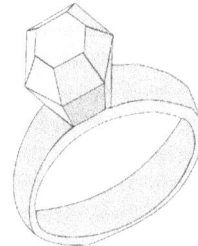

el pendiente
*ehl-pehn-dee-**ehn**-tay*
earring

11 **once** ohn-say
eleven

12 **doce** *doh*-say
twelve

13 **trece** *tray*-say
thirteen

14 **catorce** *kah*-*tohr*-say
fourteen

15 **quince** *keen*-say
fifteen

Teaching Tips:

- It's easy for children to learn numbers in order. It is much more difficult for them to be able to say them out-of-order. Make sure you help your daughter practice their numbers both ways.

Actividad Uno

Count the different objects in Spanish, then write the number in the box.

Actividad Dos

Color the picture according the codes at the bottom of the page.

12

11

15   15

11

14

13

---

color key

once - azul	catorce - negro
doce - verde	quince - rojo
trece - anaranjado	

Actividad Tres

Match the number to the word in Spanish. Then, write Spanish number in the space provided.

15

| doce | _____ |

13

| catorce | _____ |

11

| trece | _____ |

12

| quince | _____ |

14

| once | _____ |

Actividad Cuatro

Counting in Twos and Fives

Practice your Spanish number by counting by twos, and fives. By doing this, you'll be able to remember all of the number more quickly. You can practice by counting your toys and grouping them first into sets of twos, and then by fives. Have fun!

> 2, 4, 6, 8, 10, 12, 14!

Actividad Cinco

Playing Dress up

What you will need:
any jewelry that you have
any jewelry that your mother will let you borrow
fancy clothes

What to do:
1. Put on some jewelry and fancy clothes.
2. Go to your mom or dad and describe all of the *joyas* that you have on.
3. Change your *joyas* and outfit.
4. Go back to your mom or dad and describe your *joyas* again.
5. Continue as long as you are having fun. Make sure to use your Spanish!

Lección 4

Polite Fairies

Vocabulary:

la hada *lah-**hah**-dah*
fairy

la ala *lah-**ah**-lah*
wing

el polvo mágico
*ehl-**pohl**-voh-**mah**-hee-koh*
magic dust

la varita *lah-vahr-**ee**-tah*
wand

Fun Phrases:

¡mucho gusto!	*moo*-choh-**goo**-stoh	nice to meet you
perdón	*pehr-**dohn***	excuse me
¡buen apetito!	*booehn-ah-pay-**tee**-toh*	have a good meal
¡salud!	*sah-**lood***	bless you (said after a sneeze)

Actividad Uno

 Look at the pictures below. Draw a line from each picture to the correct phrase in Spanish.

¡salud!

¡mucho gusto!

¡buen apetito!

Actividad Dos

Please help the fairy find her way to her *varita*. As you pass each person on the maze, make sure you say *perdón,* to be polite.

Actividad Tres

Look at each picture below. Draw a line under your favorite item and say its name in Spanish. Next, draw a circle around your least favorite item and say its name in Spanish. Finally, circle your mother's or father's favorite item in *azul* and say its name in Spanish.

Actividad Cuatro

I'm a Fairy

Dress up as a fairy and practice all of your favorite polite Spanish phrase. Say things like *"¡buen apetito!"* before your afternoon snack. Be creative; if you don't have a fairy costume, use some paper and make yourself some wings. Also, you can create a wand out of an empty paper towel roll and paper. Have fun!

Actividad Cinco

Fairy and Dress Up Bingo

What you will need:
the bingo cards and calling cards from the appendix of this book
a marker for the bingo cards - pennies or small stones
a hat or cap

What to do:
1. Your mother or father can cut the calling cards from the back of the book and put inside a hat.
2. One by one they will draw one piece of paper from the hat and say the word on the paper in Spanish.
3. Each time you hear a word, you look at your bingo card and try to find the picture. Place a marker on the spot if you have a match.
4. When you get 5 in a row, you win and you can shout out "BINGO!"
5. Try playing with a friend or a sibling and see who can win first!

BINGO!

BINGO

Lección 5
Baby Animals

Vocabulary:

el gatito
*ehl-gah-**tee**-toh*
kitten

el perrito
*ehl-pehr-**ree**-toh*
puppy

el becerro
*ehl-beh-**sehr**-roh*
calf

el polluelo
*ehl-poh-yoo-**ay**-loh*
chick

el potro
*ehl-**poh**-troh*
foal

dieciséis 16
*dee-ay-see-**says***
sixteen

diecisiete 17
*dee-ay-see-see-**ay**-tay*
seventeen

dieciocho 18
*dee-ay-see-**oh**-choh*
eighteen

diecinueve 19
*dee-ay-see-noo-**ay**-vay*
nineteen

veinte 20
***vayin**-tay*
twenty

Actividad Uno

¡*Hola!* Look at the picture below. How many of my *perrito* friends can you find? Try to find 20. As you find each one, circle it in *rojo* and count each one in Spanish.

Actividad Dos

Use your crayon and connect all of the dots to finish this picture. As you connect the dots say each number in Spanish!

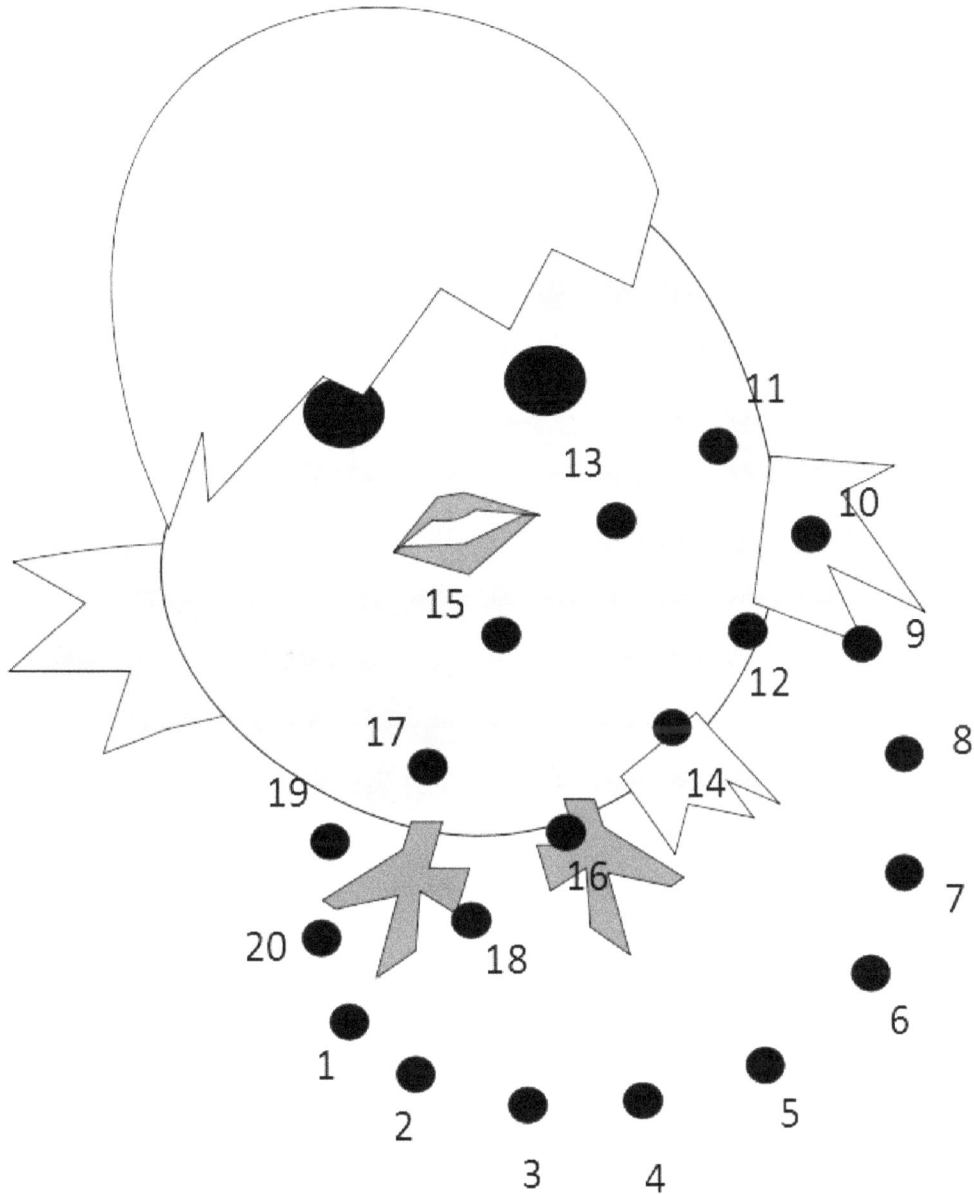

11
13
10
9
8
12
15
14
17
7
19
16
20
18
6
1
5
2
3 4

Actividad Tres

Count the pictures below in Spanish, and then circle the correct number.

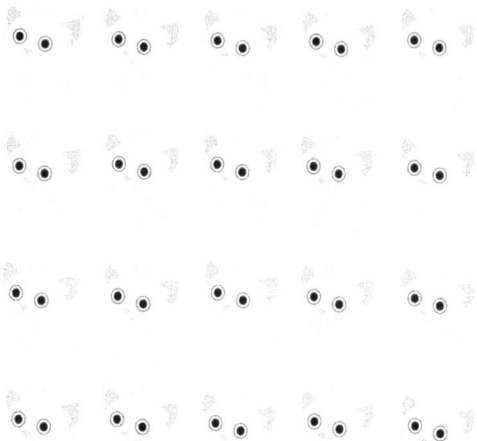

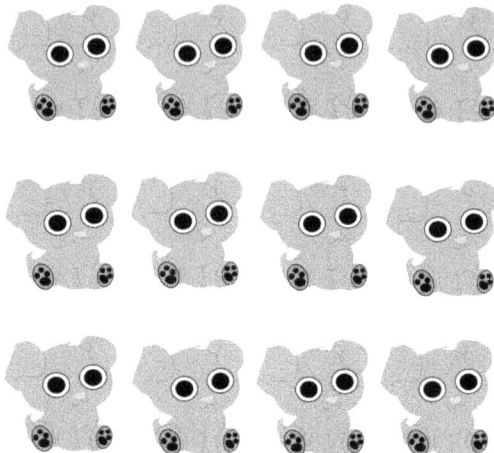

20	19	18

15	14	12

12	11	13

12	13	11

Challenge:

Start a collection of objects! Brainstorm with your parent about different things that could be in your collection (dolls, sea shells, pencils, stamps, postcards). After gathering the objects for your collection, count the number of items in your collection in Spanish. Try to find at least 20 for your collection.

Actividad Cuatro

Pet Masks

What you will need:
paper plates
scissors
glue
crayons
yarn

What to do:
1. Ask your mom or dad to help you draw a baby animal face on a paper plate.
2. Cut out and color the mask.
3. Tie yarn on it so that you can wear it.
4. Pretend to be that animal and show all of your friends. Teach them the pet's name in Spanish.

Actividad Cinco

A Dice Game

What you will need:
dice (3 or 4)
paper
pencil

What to do:
1. Roll the dice and count in Spanish how many dots you have.
2. Let the next person roll the dice and then they will count how many dots they have in Spanish.
3. Write down on the piece of paper who won that round and keep playing until one person wins 10 games.

Challenge:
Learn to count higher in Spanish and play the game with four dice.
21 - veintiuno   22 - veintidós   23 - veintitrés   24 - veinticuatro

Lección 6
Fun Sports

Vocabulary:

el fútbol
*ehl-**foot**-ball*
soccer

el ciclismo
*ehl-see-**klees**-moh*
cycling

la natación
*lah-nah-tah-see-**ohn***
swimming

el patinaje sobre hielo
*ehl-pah-tee-**nah**-hay-**soh**-bray-ee-**ay**-loh*
ice skating

la gimnasia
*lah-heem-nah-**see**-ah*
gymnastics

el tenis
*ehl-**tay**-nees*
tennis

Fun Phrases:

juego	*hoo-**ay**-goh*	I play
juegas	*hoo-**ay**-gahs*	you play

Teaching Tips:

- When you say you play a sport in Spanish, you usually need to put 'al' in front of the sport's name.
- Please note that a + el = al
- Here are some example sentences:

    Juego al tenis. - I play tennis.
    Juegas al fútbol. - You play soccer.

Actividad Uno

Draw a line from the picture, to the sport name in Spanish.

el ciclismo

la gimnasia

el patinaje sobre hielo

la natación

le tenis

Actividad Dos

Circle the six differences between the two pictures. As you find each difference count the number in Spanish.

Actividad Tres

Answer the questions below about the sports that you play. Circle *sí* for yes and *no* for no.

1. Do you like to play *"fútbol"*?	*sí*	*no*
2. Have you ever played *"tenis"*?	*sí*	*no*
3. Do you like *"ciclismo"*?	*sí*	*no*
4. Do you like to watch *"patinaje sobre hielo"*?	*sí*	*no*

Now, draw a picture of your favorite sport. Write the name of the sport on the line below the picture frame.

Actividad Cuatro

Sports Charades

What you will need:

paper
pencils
cap or hat

What to do:

1. Write down each sport name on a small piece of paper.
2. Fold each piece of paper and place it in the hat.
3. Draw a piece of paper out of the hat and act it out.
4. Everyone will guess what you are acting out, saying the name in Spanish.
5. Change rolls and keep on playing.

Challenge:

Make complete sentences with guess what sport the person is acting out. You can say things like: *Juegas al fútbol.*

Actividad Cinco

Tennis Numbers

What you will need:

10 tennis balls or another type of small ball
paper
tape
scissors
2 hats or caps

13

What to do:

1. Cut out 10 small pieces of paper and write one number on each piece of paper (11 to 20).
2. Tape one piece of paper to each ball.
3. Put all of the balls in one hat and put the other hat across the room.
4. Pull out one ball at a time and say the number in Spanish, then throw it into the other hat. If you make it, you score a point. Good Luck!

Lección 7

Dance Time

Vocabulary:

el ballet *ehl-bah-lay*
ballet

las zapatillas de ballet
lahs-sah-pah-tee-yahs-day-bah-lay
ballet shoes

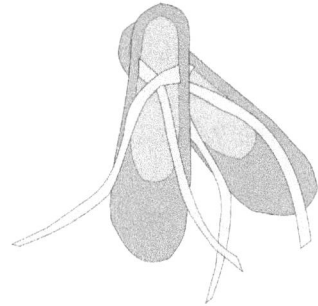

el leotardo
ehl-lay-oh-tar-doh
leotard

el claqué
ehl-klah-kay
tap dance

la danza jazz
lah-dahn-sah-yas
jazz dance

Fun Phrases:

bailo	*bah-**ee**-loh*	I dance
bailas	*bah-**ee**-lahs*	you dance
bailar	*bah-ee-**lahr***	to dance
quiero	*kee-**eh**-roh*	I want
quieres	*kee-**eh**-rehs*	you want
hacer	*ah-**sehr***	to make/to do
la danza	*lah-**dahn**-sah*	dance

Challenge:

- You can help your child form questions using the new verbs listed above:

    ¿Qué quieres hacer? - What do you want to do?

- Remember to teach these lessons as slowly or as quickly as your child needs. If your child is not ready for this challenge, you can always come back to it at a later time.

41

Actividad Uno

Look at the picture of the girl at her dance recital. Color all of the parts of the picture according to the color key below.

12

15

16   11

18

17

13

20

doce	rojo	once	negro
diecisiete	blanco	dieciocho	azul
trece	verde	quince	anaranja-do
dieciséis	negro	veinte	rojo

42

Actividad Dos

Answer the questions by drawing a picture in the box below each question or circling the answer. (*qué*=what; *cuál*=which)

1. *¿Qué quieres hacer?*

2. Draw your perfect *leotardo*. Design it anyway you want!

3. *Quieres bailar?*   *sí*   *no*

4. *Cuál danza?* Draw yourself performing the dance in the box.

Actividad Tres

Can you help me explain what I want to do and what I don't want to do? Circle the correct Spanish sentence for each picture.

Quiero bailar.

No quiero bailar.

Quiero jugar al fútbol.

No quiero jugar al fútbol.

Quiero bailar.

No quiero bailar.

Actividad Cuatro

Crazy Dancing

What you will need:
CD player or radio
dance outfit or some fun clothes

What to do:
1. Dress up in your favorite dance outfit.
2. Say "*Quiero bailar!*" so that your parent can start the music playing.
3. After a little while, they will turn off the music.
4. When you want them to start the music again, tell them that you want to dance in Spanish again.
5. Keep on dancing and having fun!

Challenge:
Reverse the game and say "*No quiero bailar!*" when you want your parents to turn off the music.

Actividad Cinco

My Book of Wants

What you will need:
old magazines
scissors
glue stick
paper
yarn

What to do:
1. With your mom or dad's help, create a little booklet out of paper by folding paper in half and fastening it with yarn.
2. On the front write: *Quiero*... (I want...)
3. Look through magazines and cut pictures of things you would like to have one day.
4. You can also draw pictures of things you want.

Lección 8
A Day at the Beach

Vocabulary:

la playa
*lah-**plah**-yah*
beach

la pelota de playa
*lah-pay-**loh**-tah-day-**plah**-yah*
beach ball

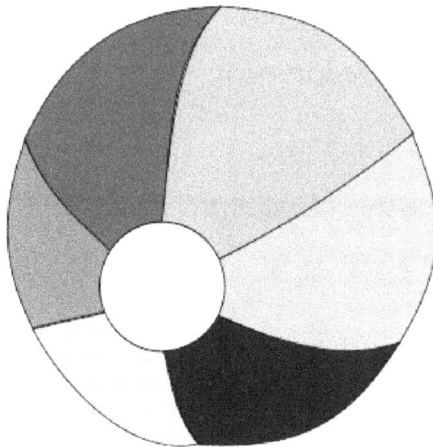

el mar
ehl-mahr
sea

la concha
*lah-**kohn**-chah*
shell

las gafas de sol
*lahs-**gah**-fahs-day-sohl*
sunglasses

la arena
*lah-ah-**ray**-nah*
sand

el castillo de arena
*ehl-kah-**stee**-yoh-day-ah-**ray**-nah*
sandcastle

Fun Phrases:

nado	**nah**-doh	I swim
nadas	**nah**-dahs	you swim

Teaching Tips:

- As your child learns new Spanish vocabulary, try to have them remember the article with the noun.

    el - masculine or *la* - feminine

Actividad Uno

Come join me at the beach! Look at the picture below. Point to items in the picture and say their name in Spanish. Each time you say a name in Spanish, color the object.

48

Actividad Dos

Draw a line from the phrase in English to the phrase in Spanish. Then, draw a picture describing the phrase.

nado

I swim

you swim

nadas

I swim

you swim

Actividad Tres

Draw a line from the picture to the correct word in Spanish. Make sure to say the Spanish word out loud as you are drawing the line.

la pelota de playa

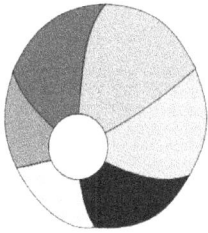

la concha

la playa

la arena

el mar

Actividad Cuatro

Counting *Conchas*

What you will need:

many *conchas* or a trip to the beach
bucket

What to do:
Option 1:
Take a trip to a beach. Pick up as many shells as you can find and put them in your bucket. Every time you pick one up, count it in Spanish.

Option 2:
Take all of the shells that you have collected on a previous trip to the beach and give them to your parents. Let them hide the shells around your house or backyard. You can then search for the *conchas*. Every time you find a shell count it in Spanish.

Actividad Cinco

A Sandy Picture

What you will need:

a little sand
paper
markers, crayons or paint
glue stick

What to do:
1. Make your own beach picture.
2. Draw all of the items that are listed in this lesson (get your parent to help you if you need help). As you draw each object, say its name in Spanish.
3. Color all of the items except for the sand.
4. Rub the glue stick on the part of the picture that is sand.
5. Sprinkle sand on the glue and let dry.
6. Dust off remaining sand and hang up your picture. Every time you walk by your picture, point to the items and say their names in Spanish.

Lección 9
Cooking in the Kitchen

Vocabulary:

la panadera
*lah-pah-nah-**day**-rah*
baker

la cocinera
*lah-koh-see-**nay**-rah*
cook

el desayuno
*ehl-dehs-ah-**yoo**-noh*
breakfast

el almuerzo
*ehl-ahl-**mooehr**-soh*
lunch

la cena
*lah-**say**-nah*
dinner

el postre
*ehl-**pohs**-tray*
dessert

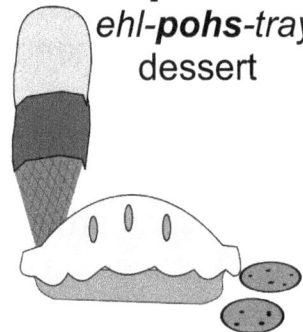

Fun Phrases:

cocino	*koh-**see**-noh*	I cook
cocinas	*koh-**see**-nahs*	you cook
la cocina	*lah-koh-**see**-nah*	kitchen

Challenge:

If you feel like your daughter is ready for some grammar, you can briefly introduce the past tense in Spanish. Spanish has two different past tenses. The one that is introduced here is called preterite. Generally, it is used to describe an action that has been completed.

There are 3 classes of verbs in Spanish. They are based on their endings -ar, -er and -ir. I cook - cocinar is an -ar verb.

To form the preterite tense take off the infinitive ending –ar, -er, or –ir and then add the preterite ending. -é for –ar verbs and -í for –er and –ir verbs for the first person singular (I). To conjugate for the second person singular (you), again take off the ending of the verb and then add –aste for –ar verbs and –iste for –er and –ir verbs.

cocinar —> cocinar —>cociné (I cooked)
cocinar —>cocinar —>cocinaste (you cooked)

53

Actividad Uno

Circle the correct word for each picture.

la cena	el desayuno

el almuerzo	la cena

el desayuno	el almuerzo

Actividad Dos

Who is cooking *desayuno*? Trace the lines to figure out who is cooking *desayuno*. Then, on the line at the bottom of the page, write the name of the person who is cooking breakfast and then rewrite the whole sentence.

María

Rosella

Linda

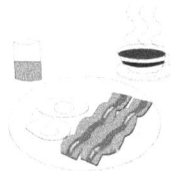

_____ cocina. (cooks)

_____

Actividad Tres

Ask your mom or dad to help you read these questions. Then, circle your answer for each question.

Have you ever made your own *almuerzo*?

sí   *no*

Which is your favorite meal of the day?

la cena   el desayuno   el almuerzo

Which of these do you help your parents to make?

el desayuno   el postre

Which would you rather be?

la panadera   la cocinera

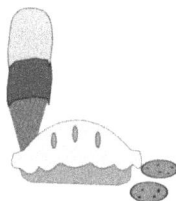

Actividad Cuatro

Which Meal?

What you will need:
Play food or pictures of food
paper bag

What to do:
1. Put your play food into the paper bag and shake it up.
2. Take one piece out of the bag and say for which meal you would eat it. For example: If you take an egg out of the bag, you can say, "*desayuno.*"

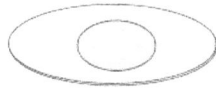

Note: Of course some food can be eaten at more than one meal, that's okay, just pick one.

Actividad Cinco

Cooking with Mom

What you will need:
a simple recipe that you can cook with your mother or father
any ingredients and/or supplies you need to make your recipe

What to do:
1. Start helping your mom cook the recipe. When you are helping say, "*Cocino.*"
2. When your mother takes over for some steps of the recipe, say, "*Cocinas.*"
3. Keep saying both sentences as you finish cooking the recipe.

Lección 10

Paper Dolls

Vocabulary:

la camisa
*lah-kah-**mee**-sah*
shirt

los pantalones
*lohs-pahn-tah-**loh**-nehs*
pants

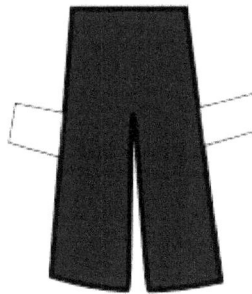

el vestido
*ehl-vehs-**tee**-doh*
dress

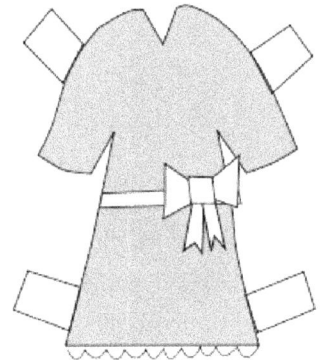

la falda
*lah-**fahl**-dah*
skirt

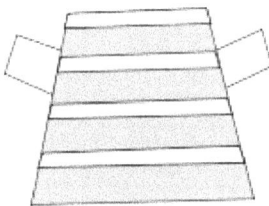

el abrigo
*ehl-ah-**bree**-goh*
coat

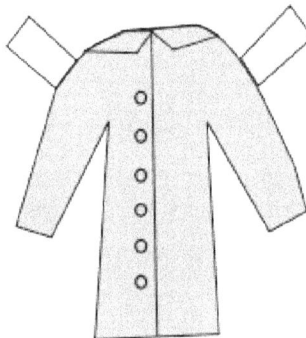

el sombrero
*ehl-sohm-**bray**-roh*
hat

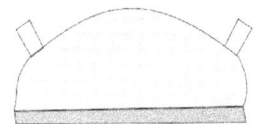

Actividad Uno

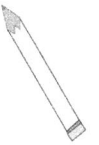

Opps, my friend Laure got caught out in the rain and now her clothes are all wet. Can you draw her some new clothes? As you draw the clothes, say their names in Spanish.

Actividad Dos

In the appendix are paper dolls and clothes that you can use for this activity. Cut the pieces out, color them, then come back to this page. Use your doll on this scene. Describe the clothes the dolls are wearing.

Challenge: Speak for each doll telling the other doll what they are wearing. You can use the phrases: *llevo* (***yay***-*voh*) for 'I am wearing' and *llevas* (***yay***-*vahs*) for 'you are wearing'.

Actividad Tres

Fill in the missing letters and then draw a line from the picture to the correct Spanish word.

la f_lda

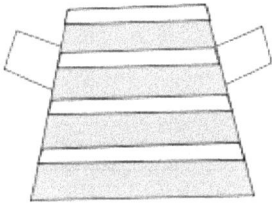

los panta_on_s

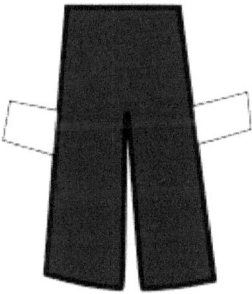

el ab_i_o

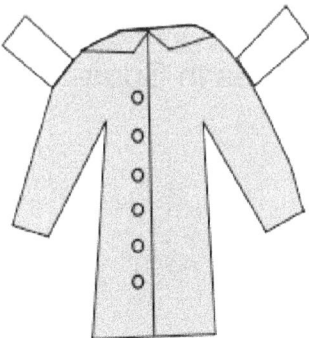

la ca_isa

Actividad Cuatro

Matching Game

You will need:
the matching cards from the back of this workbook
scissors

What to do:
1. Turn the cards upside-down.
2. Turn over two at a time to see if you have a pair of the picture and the correct word in Spanish. If so, put them in a pile; if not, turn them back over and try again.

Challenge:
Every time you make a match of cards, make a complete sentence with the word in Spanish!

Actividad Cinco

Pulling it Together

You will need:
any toys or objects that you have which you learned their names in this workbook - stuffed baby animals, fairy wings, etc.
backpack

What to do:
1. Put all of the toys and objects in your backpack.
2. Surprise your parents or grandparents. Tell them you have something to show them.
3. Then, one by one, take out each object and say their names in Spanish. Try to make sentences too, if you would like to try.

Appendices

My Learning Slide

Every time you finish a lección in the book,
color a section of the learning slide.

Three cheers for

Félicitations!
Congratulations!
You have successfully finished
More Spanish for Little Girls.

English to Spanish Dictionary

artist	la artista	*lah-ahr-**tees**-tah*
baker	la panadera	*lah-pah-nah-**day**-rah*
ballet	el ballet	*ehl-bah-**lay***
ballet shoes	las zapatillas de ballet	*lahs-sah-pah-**tee**-yahs-day-bah-**lay***
beach	la playa	*lah-**plah**-yah*
beach ball	la pelota de pla-ya	*lah-pay-**loh**-tah-day-**plah**-yah*
bless you	salud	*sah-**lood***
bracelet	la pulsera	*lah-pool-**say**-rah*
breakfast	el desayuno	*ehl-dehs-ah-**yoo**-noh*
calf	el becerro	*ehl-beh-**sehr**-roh*
chick	el polluelo	*ehl-poh-yoo-**ay**-loh*
coat	el abrigo	*ehl-ah-**bree**-goh*
cook	la cocinera	*lah-koh-see-**nay**-rah*

cycling	el ciclismo	*ehl-see-**klees**-moh*
dance	la danza	*lah-**dahn**-sah*
dessert	el postre	*ehl-**pohs**-tray*
dinner	la cena	*lah-**say**-nah*
dress	el vestido	*ehl-vehs-**tee**-doh*
earring	el pendiente	*ehl-pehn-dee-**ehn**-tay*
ears	las orejas	*lahs-oh-**ray**-hahs*
eighteen	dieciocho	*dee-ay-see-**oh**-choh*
eleven	once	***ohn**-say*
excuse me	perdón	*pehr-**dohn***
eyes	los ojos	*lohs-**oh**-hohs*
face	la cara	*lah-**kah**-rah*
fairy	la hada	*lah-**hah**-dah*
fifteen	quince	***keen**-say*

football	el fútbol	*ehl-**foot**-ball*
foal	el potro	*ehl-**poh**-troh*
fourteen	catorce	*kah-**tohr**-say*
gymnastics	la gimnasia	*lah-heem-nah-**see**-ah*
hair	el pelo	*ehl-**pay**-loh*
hat	el sombrero	*ehl-sohm-**bray**-roh*
have a good meal	buen apetito	*booehn-ah-pay-**tee**-toh*
I am angry	estoy enojada	*eh-**stoy**-ay-noh-**hah**-dah*
I am crazy	estoy loca	*eh-**stoy-loh**-kah*
I am happy	estoy feliz	*eh-**stoy**-fay-**lees***
I am sad	estoy triste	*eh-**stoy-trees**-tay*
I cook	cocino	*koh-**see**-noh*
I dance	bailo	*bah-**ee**-loh*

I play	juego	*hoo-**ay**-goh*
I swim	nado	***nah**-doh*
I want	quiero	*kee-**eh**-roh*
ice skating	el patinaje sobre hielo	*ehl-pah-tee-**nah**-hay-**soh**-bray-ee-**ay**-loh*
jazz dance	la danza jazz	*lah-**dahn**-sah-yas*
jewelry	las joyas	*lahs-**hoh**-yahs*
kitchen	la cocina	*lah-koh-**see**-nah*
kitten	el gatito	*ehl-gah-**tee**-toh*
leotard	el leotardo	*ehl-lay-oh-**tar**-doh*
lunch	el almuerzo	*ehl-ahl-**mooehr**-soh*
magic dust	el polvo mágico	*ehl-**pohl**-voh-**mah**-hee-koh*
maybe	quizás	***kee**-sahs*
mouth	la boca	*lah-**boh**-kah*

necklace	el collar	*ehl-koh-**lahr***
no	no	*noh*
nose	la nariz	*lah-nah-**rees***
nice to meet you	mucho gusto	***moo**-choh-**goo**-stoh*
nineteen	diecinueve	*dee-ay-see-noo-**ay**-vay*
paint	la pintura	*lah-peen-**too**-rah*
paint brush	el cepillo de pintura	*ehl-say-**pee**-yoh-day-peen-**too**-rah*
painter	la pintora	*lah-peen-**tohr**-ah*
pants	los pantalones	*lohs-pahn-tah-**loh**-nehs*
pencil	el lápiz	*ehl-**pah**-pees*
puppy	el perrito	*ehl-pehr-**ree**-toh*
ring	el anillo	*ehl-ah-**nee**-yoh*
sand	la arena	*lah-ah-**ray**-nah*
sandcastle	el castillo de arena	*ehl-kah-**stee**-yoh-day-ah-**ray**-nah*

sculptor	la escultora	*lah-ehs-kool-**toh**-rah*
sea	el mar	*ehl-mahr*
seventeen	diecisiete	*dee-ay-see-see-**ay**-tay*
shell	la concha	*lah-**kohn**-chah*
shirt	la camisa	*lah-kah-**mee**-sah*
sixteen	dieciséis	*dee-ay-see-**says***
skirt	la falda	*lah-**fahl**-dah*
sunglasses	las gafas de sol	*lahs-**gah**-fahs-day-sohl*
swimming	la natación	*lah-nah-tah-see-**ohn***
tap dance	el claqué	*ehl-klah-**kay***
tennis	el tenis	*ehl-**tay**-nees*
thirteen	trece	***tray**-say*
to dance	bailar	*bah-ee-**lahr***
to make/to do	hacer	*ah-**sehr***

twelve	doce	*doh-say*
twenty	veinte	*vayin-tay*
very	muy	*moo-ee*
wand	la varita	*lah-vahr-ee-tah*
wing	la ala	*lah-ah-lah*
yes	sí	*see*
you cook	cocinas	*koh-see-nahs*
you dance	bailas	*bah-ee-lahs*
you play	juegas	*hoo-ay-gahs*
you swim	nadas	*nah-dahs*
you want	quieres	*kee-eh-rehs*

Spanish to English Dictionary

el abrigo	*ehl-ah-**bree**-goh*	coat
la ala	*lah-**ah**-lah*	wing
el almuerzo	*ehl-ahl-**mooehr**-soh*	lunch
el anillo	*ehl-ah-**nee**-yoh*	ring
la arena	*lah-ah-**ray**-nah*	sand
la artista	*lah-ahr-**tees**-tah*	artist
bailar	*bah-ee-**lahr***	to dance
bailo	*bah-**ee**-loh*	I dance
el ballet	*ahl-bah-**lay***	ballet
el becerro	*ehl-beh-**sehr**-roh*	calf
la boca	*lah-**boh**-kah*	mouth
buen apetito	*booehn-ah-pay-**tee**-toh*	have a good meal
la camisa	*lah-kah-**mee**-sah*	shirt

la cara	lah-**kah**-rah	face
el castillo de arena	ehl-kah-**stee**-yoh-day-ah-**ray**-nah	sandcastle
catorce	kah-**tohr**-say	fourteen
la cena	lah-**say**-nah	dinner
el cepillo de pintura	ehl-say-**pee**-yoh-day-peen-**too**-rah	paint brush
el ciclismo	ehl-see-**klees**-moh	cycling
el claqué	ehl-klah-**kay**	tap dance
la cocina	lah-koh-**see**-nah	kitchen
la cocinera	lah-koh-see-**nay**-rah	cook
cocinas	koh-**see**-nahs	you cook
cocino	koh-**see**-noh	I cook
el collar	ehl-koh-**lahr**	necklace
la concha	lah-**kohn**-chah	shell
la danza	lah-**dahn**-sah	dance

la danza jazz	lah-**dahn**-sah-yas	jazz dance
desayuno	ehl-dehs-ah-**yoo**-noh	breakfast
diecinueve	dee-ay-see-noo-**ay**-vay	nineteen
dieciocho	lahs-oh-**ray**-hahs	eighteen
diecisiete	dee-ay-see-see-**ay**-tay	seventeen
doce	doh-**say**	twelve
la escultora	lah-ehs-kool-**toh**-rah	sculptor
estoy enojada	eh-**stoy**-**ay**-noh-hah-dah	I am angry
estoy feliz	eh-**stoy**-fay-**lees**	I am happy
estoy loca	eh-**stoy**-**loh**-kah	I am crazy
estoy triste	eh-**stoy**-**trees**-tay	I am sad
la falda	lah-**fahl**-dah	skirt
el fútbol	ehl-**foot**-ball	football

las gafas de sol	lahs-**gah**-fahs-day-sohl	sunglasses
el gatito	ehl-gah-**tee**-toh	kitten
la gimnasia	lah-heem-nah-**see**-ah	gymnastics
hacer	ah-**sehr**	to make/to do
la hada	lah-**hah**-dah	fairy
las joyas	lah-**hoh**-yahs	jewelry
juegas	hoo-**ay**-gahs	you play
juego	hoo-**ay**-goh	I play
el lápiz	ehl-**pah**-pees	pencil
el leotardo	ehl-lay-oh-**tar**-doh	leotard
el mar	ehl-mahr	sea
mucho gusto	**moo**-choh-**goo**-stoh	nice to meet you
muy	moo-**ee**	very
nadas	**nah**-dahs	you swim

nado	*nah*-doh	I swim
la nariz	lah-nah-***rees***	nose
la natación	lah-nah-tah-see-***ohn***	swimming
no	noh	no
los ojos	lohs-***oh***-hohs	eyes
once	***ohn***-say	eleven
las orejas	lahs-oh-***ray***-hahs	ears
la panadera	lah-pah-nah-***day***-rah	baker
los pantalones	lohs-pahn-tah-***loh***-nehs	pants
el patinaje sobre hielo	ehl-pah-tee-***nah***-hay-***soh***-bray-ee-***ay***-loh	ice skating
el pelo	ehl-***pay***-loh	hair
la pelota de pla-ya	lah-pay-***loh***-tah-day-***plah***-yah	beach ball
el pendiente	ehl-pehn-dee-***ehn***-tay	earring

el perrito	*ehl-pehr-**ree**-toh*	puppy
la pintora	*lah-peen-**tohr**-ah*	painter
la pintura	*lah-peen-**too**-rah*	paint
la playa	*lah-**plah**-yah*	beach
el polluelo	*ehl-poh-yoo-**ay**-loh*	chick
el polvo mágico	*ehl-**pohl**-voh-**mah**-hee-koh*	magic dust
el postre	*ehl-**pohs**-tray*	dessert
el potro	*ehl-**poh**-troh*	foal
la pulsera	*lah-pool-**say**-rah*	bracelet
quieres	*kee-**eh**-rehs*	you want
quiero	*kee-**eh**-roh*	I want
quince	***keen**-say*	fifteen
salud	*sah-**lood***	bless you
sí	*see*	yes

el sombrero	*ehl-sohm-**bray**-roh*	hat
el tenis	*ehl-**tay**-nes*	tennis
trece	***tray**-say*	thirteen
la varita	*lah-vahr-**ee**-tah*	wand
veinte	***vayin**-tay*	twenty
el vestido	*ehl-vehs-**tee**-doh*	dress
las zapatillas de ballet	*lahs-sah-pah-**tee**-yahs-day-bah-**lay***	ballet shoes

Bingo

What you will need:
- Bingo cards – in this booklet.
- A hat or a cap.
- Something to cover up the squares on the cards, like dry beans or pennies.

What to do:
1. Cut out the cards on page 87, fold them and put them into a hat.
2. Draw one strip of paper out and say the word with the letter.
3. The children will cover up the word that they heard.
4. Repeat 4 and 5 until there is a winner!

B	I	N	G	O
		free square		

B	I	N	G	O
		free square		

B	I	N	G	O
		free square		

Cards for Bingo

B - la hada	B - el polvo mágico	B - las joyas	B - la pintura	B - la pulsera
B - la ala	B - el pendiente	B - la varita	B - la collar	B - el anillo
I - la hada	I - el polvo mágico	I - las joyas	I - la pintura	I - la pulsera
I - la ala	I - el pendiente	I - la varita	I - la collar	I - el anillo
N - la hada	N - el polvo mágico	N - las joyas	N - la pintura	N - la pulsera
N - la ala	N - el pendiente	N - la varita	N - la collar	N - el anillo
G - la hada	G - el polvo mágico	G - las joyas	G - la pintura	G - la pulsera
G - la ala	G - el pendiente	G - la varita	G - la collar	G - el anillo
O - la hada	O - el polvo mágico	O - las joyas	O - la pintura	O - la pulsera
O - la ala	O - el pendiente	O - la varita	O - la collar	O - el anillo

Matching Game

What to do:
1. Cut out the following cards. Paste them onto card board for stability if you would like.
2. Turn the cards upside-down.
3. Turn over two at a time to see if you have a pair of the picture and the correct word in Spanish.

la varita

el cepillo de pintura

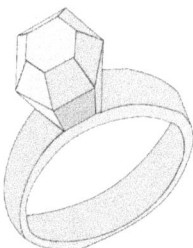

el anillo

la hada

el potro

la gimnasia

la danza
jazz

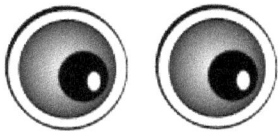

los ojos

la cocinera

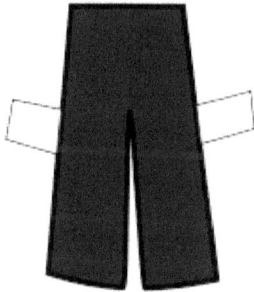

los pantalones

la concha

Paper Dolls

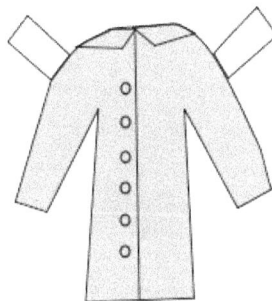
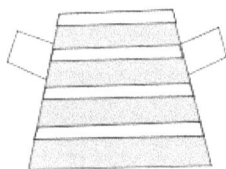

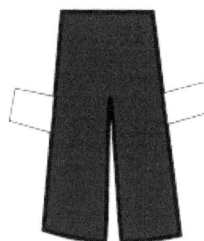

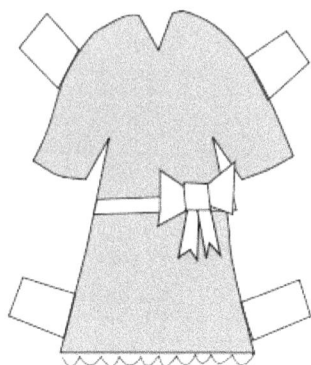

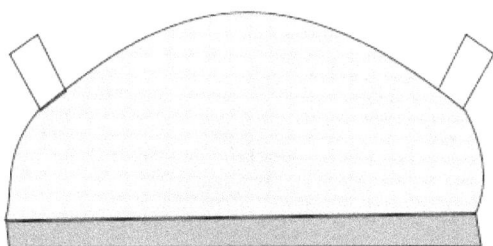
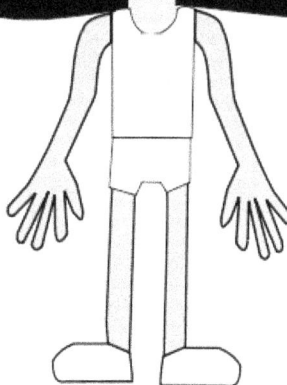

www.ingramcontent.com/pod-product-compliance
Lightning Source LLC
Chambersburg PA
CBHW062106090426
42741CB00015B/3346